Fifteen Sketches and Mini-dramas

Edited and annotated by
Wilfried Proges and Thomas Tepe

Ernst Klett Verlag
Stuttgart Düsseldorf Leipzig

Fifteen Sketches and Mini-dramas

Herausgegeben und annotiert von
Wilfried Proges und Thomas Tepe

1. Auflage 1 5 4 3 2 1 | 2008 07 06 05 04

Alle Drucke dieser Auflage können im Unterricht nebeneinander benutzt werden. Die letzte Zahl bezeichnet das Jahr dieses Druckes.

Internetadresse: www.klett-verlag.de

Redaktion: Inge Schäfer, Verlagsredakteurin

Umschlagbild: Sepp Buchegger
Druck: Mediendruck Unterland, Flein
Printed in Germany.
ISBN 3-12-577930-8

9 783125 779303

Contents

The arrangement of the texts in *Setting the scene* is alphabetical (*Buis* to *Ullom*).

Introduction

Dear theatre-loving students,

"All the world's a stage", Shakespeare once said. Your school should be one as well! If it isn't, however, this collection of contemporary sketches and mini-dramas will help you to turn it into a playhouse where you are the performing company. This collection will make you familiar with the basics of drama as a literary form, but more importantly it will enable you to become active members of the fascinating world of the theatre as actors and actresses, stage directors, sound technicians, lighting designers, prompters, critics and, last but not least, members of the audience. In any or all of these capacities, you and your teacher can become involved in the happy, the sad, the horrible, the funny and the incredible events presented in these texts.

Some of the texts offered have been written by well-known dramatists (Friel, Pinter, Saunders, etc.), whereas others are by writers who work in the educational field (Mauro, McFarland, Ullom, etc.). Some of the playwrights live and work in the British Isles, and some on the other side of the Atlantic. Thus, this collection contains examples of British as well as American English (cf. Friel's *American Welcome*) that demonstrate differences between the two varieties of English. The themes of these sketches are very diverse, but all of them deal with topics that you can certainly relate to: personal relationships; political, social and educational issues; the world of jobs, etc.

Wherever possible, a short note on the playwright has been given. The *Annotations* explain words, phrases and names which the editors thought you might not be familiar with.

If, while working with this collection of sketches and mini-dramas, you find the enterprise a worthwhile theatrical adventure, then this book will have served its purpose.

We wish you all an enjoyable series of dramatic lessons.

The editors (Wilfried Proges & Thomas Tepe)

Getting started

Jest a Moment

from: Fred Metcalf

a) *Boy:* Come out for a meal with me.
Girl: I can't.
Boy: But I don't want to eat on my own.
Girl: I can't.
Boy: And I love to talk to you.
Girl: I can't.
Boy: I'm going to the Ritz.
Girl: I can.

b) *A:* Hey, your dog's just eaten my hat!
B: Don't worry, he likes hats.
A: But it was my best hat!
B: It doesn't matter. All hats are the same to him.
A: Are you trying to annoy me?
B: What makes you say that?
A: It's your attitude.
B: It's not my 'at 'ee chewed, it's your 'at 'ee chewed!

c) *A:* I've got this terrific new job in the circus – mucking out the elephants.
B: Mucking out the elephants! How many of them?
A: Twenty-five.
B: Twenty-five elephants! How much do they pay you?
A: Ten pounds a week.
B: Ten pounds a week for mucking out twenty-five elephants! If I were you I'd chuck it all in and get a decent office job.
A: What – and give up show business?

to jest to say s.th. in order to make others laugh – 13 **to annoy s.o.** to make s.o. rather angry – 17 **to muck out** to clean out the place where animals live – 24 **to chuck it all in** (*informal*) to give up one's job

Talking about your experience with drama

(The following tasks can be tackled in a brainstorming session.)

- *Compare which dramas you have either watched or read in class or during your free time. Discuss which methods you used to understand and interpret these dramas. Compare these methods.*
- *Gather what you know about sketches or mini-dramas (which you may have become aquainted with in the media, a drama group at your school, etc.) and on this basis write dictionary definitions for these terms.*

The Question Game

W. F. Irmscher

No. 1 is on the stage, not doing much of anything.
No. 2 enters, apparently confused.

No. 2 Where am I?
No. 1 What?
No. 2 Where am I going?
No. 1 Where did you come from?
No. 2 What are you doing here?
No. 1 Why do you ask?
No. 2 Who are you, anyway?
No. 1 What's it to you?
No. 2 Why are you here?
No. 1 Me?
No. 2 Are you mad?
No. 1 What do you mean?
No. 2 Are you?
No. 1 Who do you think you are?
No. 2 Did God put you here?
No. 1 What?
No. 2 Is there a God?
No. 1 What?
No. 2 Is there?
No. 1 How should I know?
No. 2 Don't you know?
No. 1 No, of course not.
No. 2 Neither do I.

No. 2 exits, leaving No. 1 on the stage, apparently confused.

First impressions are important, aren't they?

- *As a class, have a look at the titles of all the sketches contained in this volume and, based on the titles, describe what you think each sketch will be like. Will the sketch be interesting/exciting/adventurous/thrilling/romantic?*
- *In groups of equal size, try to anticipate the theme and the plot of some of the sketches.*
- *As a class, compare your results and decide on the sketches which the majority would like to deal with.*
- *Form groups again; each group should quickly read one of the chosen sketches and complete a grid with the following categories: title, tone, theme, characters, message. Reading in this case serves the purpose of getting a first impression of the sketch. This impression will later on be intensified and possibly modified. Your grid might look like this:*

Title:	Tone:	Theme:	Characters:	Message:
"Useless but High Paying"	humorous	jobs and careers	interviewer/ applicant	criticism of political careers
...	...	...	...	...

Words which will help you to describe the tone in sketches:
(See also p. 56ff, "Vocabulary, exercises, activities".)

satirical, humorous, aggressive, funny, critical, cruel, farcical, serious, moralistic, playful, sarcastic, tragic, melodramatic, comic

Making a selection

- *Collect and compare the findings of the groups (as a class).*
- *In different groups, develop criteria which will help you to decide which sketches are worth reading in detail.*
- *As a class, discuss your suggestions and reach an agreement about which sketches you will read.*

Setting the scene

Useless but High Paying

Kirk Buis*

AT RISE: Two people are sitting at a desk.

INTERVIEWER: And tell me, Mr. Touchstone, did you have any particular type of work in mind?

CLIENT: Well, I'm looking for a job that doesn't require a lot of skill.

INTERVIEWER: I see. *(Writing)* Little skill. *(To CLIENT)* Anything else?

CLIENT: Yes, there are a few other things I'd like to have.

INTERVIEWER: Splendid. It makes it so much easier when our clients know just what they're looking for. What are these other requirements?

CLIENT: I'd like a job with no challenge to it.

INTERVIEWER: Cut and dried. Straightforward, eh? *(Writing)* No challenge. *(To CLIENT)* Yes?

CLIENT: And one that affords me a great deal of leisure time. Perhaps if I could work only three or four days a week.

INTERVIEWER: *(Writing)* Leisure ... short work week. *(To CLIENT)* How about the work day? Keep that short?

CLIENT: I didn't know if that was asking too much or not.

INTERVIEWER: Of course not! Your satisfaction is our goal. Was there anything else?

CLIENT: There was one other thing.

INTERVIEWER: And what might that be?

CLIENT: A – uh – voluptuous secretary.

* lives and writes in the USA

4 **to require** (*formal*) to need – 12 **challenge** *here*: difficulties – 13 **cut and dried** clear – **straightforward** *here*: easy to do – 15 **to afford** [ə'fɔ:d] *here*: to give – **leisure** ['leʒə] time when you are not working and can relax – 20 **goal** *here*: aim – 24 **voluptuous** [və'lʌptʃʊəs] sexually attractive

INTERVIEWER: Ah! Is that everything?

CLIENT: Yes, I think so.

INTERVIEWER: All right. Now, about the salary. What range were you thinking of?

CLIENT: Well, I've seen the new line of cars, and I was hoping for something, say, around a hundred thousand.

INTERVIEWER: Are you sure that will be enough?

CLIENT: I'm willing to trade in the old car.

INTERVIEWER: What if one of them breaks down? A second car is always handy.

CLIENT: I suppose you're right.

INTERVIEWER: Let's put down one and a quarter, minimum. How does that sound?

CLIENT: Fine! Do you think you'll be able to find anything?

INTERVIEWER: Let's take a look, shall we? *(Opens drawer, flips through folders.)* Challenging ... fulfilling ... rewarding ... ah, here we are. *(Pulls out folder.)* Useless but high paying. Let's see now. Can you throw a baseball, by any chance?

CLIENT: Not very accurately.

INTERVIEWER: Well, we'll put relief pitcher aside for now. Although there are several organizations willing to pay for very minimal talent and the hours are well within your range. Hmmm. How about network news anchor? That wouldn't be too bad. And the skill level is definitely low. Do you wear sweaters with your suits?

CLIENT: No, I don't.

INTERVIEWER: *(Disappointed)* Oh. Well, the hours are a little late, also. We'll keep looking.

CLIENT: Do you have this much trouble with all your clients?

3 **salary** money people get for doing a regular job – 5 **line** *here*: type – 8 **to trade s.th. in** to give s.th. as part of the payment for s.th. new – 10 **handy** useful – 15 **drawer** [drɔ:] box with a handle which can be pulled out from a desk or cupboard – **to flip through s.th.** to look through s.th. quickly – 16 **folder** *Akte* – **challenging** interesting or enjoyable, but difficult – **rewarding** worthwhile – 33 **accurately** ['ækjərətlı] – 20 **relief pitcher** (in baseball) a pitcher (person who throws the ball to the person supposed to hit it) who takes the place of another – 22 **within your range** what you expect – 23 **network news anchor** person who reads the news for a TV or radio station – 25 **sweater** ['swetə] pullover

INTERVIEWIER: Sometimes. But don't worry. There are still many more here. Know much about the law?

CLIENT: Not really.

INTERVIEWER: Ever gotten a ticket?

CLIENT: *(Hesitating)* No.

INTERVIEWER: Ever been stopped?

CLIENT: Well, maybe once.

INTERVIEWER: Or twice?

CLIENT: It was nothing serious.

INTERVIEWER: But no ticket?

CLIENT: No. Never.

INTERVIEWER: See! You must know something about the law!

CLIENT: I guess you're right.

INTERVIEWER: How does senior law partner sound?

CLIENT: Not bad! Not bad at all!

INTERVIEWER: Let's see. The salary is well within your range. The hours, hmmm, set your own! Ah, wait! How many dull suits do you have?

CLIENT: I try to avoid buying them.

INTERVIEWER: *(Confidentially)* Mr. Touchstone, we try to fit the job to the person, and if you don't mind my saying so, I would honestly try to persuade you against taking this position. I just can't quite picture you at two-hour lunches in a three-piece suit.

CLIENT: Oh.

INTERVIEWER: Naturally, we could arrange for you to try the position out for a week or two.

CLIENT: No. No. I think you're probably right. There are also a lot of conferences with that job too, aren't there?

INTERVIEWER: Yes, it does say that you would have to attend at least three boring meetings a week.

CLIENT: That really wasn't what I had in mind. What's that next one with a star on it?

4 **ticket** *here*: *Strafzettel* – 5 **to hesitate** to pause for a moment – 14 **senior** ['si:njə] *here:* higher in status than others – **law partner** one of the people who work in a law firm – 17 **dull** *here*: not fashionable – 22 **to persuade s.o.** to give s.o. good reasons to do s.th. – 23 **to picture** to imagine

INTERVIEWER: Hmmm. This doesn't sound too bad. In fact, I think it could be right up your alley. Power. Prestige. Little or no work. Travel possibilities. It has a modest salary, but the fringe benefits more than make up for the base pay.

CLIENT: What is it?

INTERVIEWER: Politician. How does Senator or Congressman sound?

CLIENT: Nothing higher up?

INTERVIEWER: *(Checks folder.)* Not at this time.

CLIENT: Don't they have a lot of responsibilities?

INTERVIEWER: Nothing is written down. In fact, it says, "Presence is suggested, but not mandatory." Sounds like the hours would suit you.

CLIENT: What was that about travel possibilities?

INTERVIEWER: Yes. It says, "At no cost, 'working vacation,'" that's in quotes, "can be arranged almost anywhere to," quotes again, "'facilitate trade relations.'"

CLIENT: I could do that.

INTERVIEWER: Certainly! Well, Congressman Touchstone?

CLIENT: … I'll take it!

INTERVIEWER: Wonderful! Congratulations! *(Shakes hands.)* I knew you could do it. *(CLIENT strikes "congressional" pose.)* Now, there are a few minor details. Would you rather be a Republican or a Democrat?

CLIENT: Does it make a difference?

INTERVIEWER: No. It's a formality. Let me put it this way. Would you rather own an elephant or a donkey?

CLIENT: The mess either one of them would make would be awful to clean up. Oh, what the heck, elephant.

2 **right up your alley** *(informal)* perfect for you – **prestige** [pres'ti:ʒ] – 3 **fringe benefits** additional benefits (e.g. a company car) which s.o. gets on top of the usual pay – 4 **to make up for s.th.** to compensate for s.th. – 12 **mandatory** ['mændətrɪ] required, obligatory – 17 **to facilitate** to make easier – 22 **to strike a pose** to behave as if you are s.o. else (*here*: a member of Congress) – 23 **minor** ['maɪnə] unimportant – 27 **elephant/donkey** ['dɒŋkɪ] *here*: (in the US) animals which are used as symbols for the Republican/Democratic parties – 28 **mess** chaos, dirtiness – 29 **what the heck** (*informal*) expression meaning "why not!"

INTERVIEWER: Wonderful. There is a little matter of an election, but we'll take care of that.

CLIENT: When do I start?

INTERVIEWER: Let's see. How does the first of the year sound?

CLIENT: Fine.

INTERVIEWER: Then I think that will do it, Mr. Congressman.

CLIENT: That has a nice ring to it.

INTERVIEWER: Good luck.

CLIENT: Thank you. *(CLIENT exits.)*

INTERVIEWER: *(Into telephone)* Next, please.

(Curtain)

7 **to have a nice ring to it** to sound nice and attractive

Fatal Beatings

Ben Elton and Richard Curtis*

(Schoolboy music. A formal looking tweedy gentleman with an Edinburgh accent sits at a desk. There is a knock on the door.)

HEADMASTER: Come in!!!

(A tidy, sports-jacketed man enters. MR PERKINS.)

PERKINS: Ah, good morning, Headmaster.

HEADMASTER: Ah, Mr Perkins. It was good of you to come in. I realize that you're a busy man, but I didn't feel that we could discuss this matter over the electric telephone

PERKINS: No, absolutely, Headmaster, I mean if Tommy's in some sort of trouble I'd like to nip it in the bud.

HEADMASTER: Well, quite frankly, Mr Perkins, Tommy is in trouble. Recently his behaviour has left a great deal to be desired.

PERKINS: Oh, dear me.

HEADMASTER: Yes, he takes no interest in school life whatsoever, he refuses to muck in on the sports field and it's weeks since any master received any written work from him.

PERKINS: Dear me.

HEADMASTER: Quite frankly, Mr Perkins, if he wasn't dead, I'd have him expelled.

PERKINS: I beg your pardon.

* Elton, Ben: * 1959, lives in London, studied drama at Manchester University, works as an emcee (TV and theatre)
Curtis, Richard: * 1956 in New Zealand, lives in London, writer of film scripts (chiefly comedies) e.g. *Four Weddings and a Funeral*, also wrote for Rowan Atkinson (*Mr. Bean*)

fatal causing death – 10 **to nip s.th. in the bud** (*informal*) to stop s.th. from developing further – 11 **frankly** honestly, openly – 12 **recently** during the past few days or weeks – **to leave s.th. to be desired** to be not as good as expected – 16 **to muck in** (*informal*) to work together with other people, to co-operate – 17 **master** *here*: teacher – 20 **to expel** to throw out, to force to leave

HEADMASTER: Yes, expelled. If I wasn't making allowances for the fact that your son is dead he'd be out on his ear.

PERKINS: Tommy's dead?

HEADMASTER: Yes, he's lying upstairs in sick bay now, stiff as a board and bright green. And this is, I fear, typical of his current attitude. I have pleaded with him, and so has matron, and he will make no effort.

PERKINS: Tommy's dead!

HEADMASTER: Yes, that's what's so galling – he seems to have no sense of moderation – one moment he's flying around like a paper kite, the next he's completely immovable and beginning to smell.

PERKINS: How did he die?

HEADMASTER: Well, is that important?

PERKINS: Yes, I think so.

HEADMASTER: Well, it's all got to do with the library. You see we've had some trouble recently with boys taking library books without library cards. Your son was caught and I administered a beating, during which he died. But you'll be glad to know that the ringleader has been caught, so I don't think we'll have to worry about library discipline any more. You see the library-card system ...

PERKINS: I'm sorry, you beat my son to death?

HEADMASTER: Yes, yes, so it would seem. Please, I'm not used to being interrupted. The library-card system was introduced ...

PERKINS: Exactly what happened?

HEADMASTER: Well, apparently the boys were just slipping into the library and taking the books.

PERKINS: No, during the beating.

1 **to make allowances for s.th.** to take s.th. into consideration (*berücksichtigen*) – 2 **to be out on one's ear** (*informal*) *here:* to be thrown out of school – 4 **sick bay** place where the sick are treated – 5 **current** present – 6 **to plead** [i:] **with s.o.** to ask s.o. in an emotional way to do s.th. – **matron** ['meɪtrən] *(BE)* woman who works as a nurse in a school – 7 **to make an effort** ['efət] to try hard to do s.th. – 9 **galling** ['gɔ:lɪŋ] very irritating – 10 **moderation** self-control (*Mäßigung*) – 18 **to administer** (*formal*) to give – 20 **ringleader** s.o. who leads a group in doing forbidden activities – 27 **apparently** so it seems

HEADMASTER: Oh, that, oh well, one moment he was bending over, and the next he was lying down.

PERKINS: Dead?

HEADMASTER: Deadish. Really, Mr Perkins, I'm starting to find this morbid fascination of yours with your son's death slightly disturbing. What we're talking about here is your son's attitude, and quite frankly I'm beginning to see where he gets it from.

PERKINS: At least I never beat him to death.

HEADMASTER: No, that was quite obvious to me from the day he arrived here, and I wondered then, and I wonder now, Mr Perkins, whether he might not have turned out a very different lad indeed if you had administered a few fatal beatings earlier on.

PERKINS: Are you completely mad?

HEADMASTER: Yes, I'm absolutely furious. In order to accommodate the funeral we've had to cancel afternoon school on Wednesday. I'm sorry, I have to be going.

PERKINS: This is preposterous.

HEADMASTER: Yes it is. Or rather it would be – if it were true.

PERKINS:What?

HEADMASTER: I've been joking, Mr Perkins. Forgive me, it's my strange Hibernian sense of humour. I've been having you on.

PERKINS: Oh. Thank God for that.

HEADMASTER: I wouldn't cancel afternoon school to bury that little twerp.

4 **deadish** sort of dead – 5 **morbid** having a strong interest in disease or death – **slightly** a little bit – 9 **obvious** clear – 12 **lad** *(informal, old-fashioned; still used in Scotland)* boy, young man – 14 **mad** 1. crazy, 2. very angry – 15 **furious** very angry – **to accommodate s.th**. (*formal*) *here:* to allow time for s.th. – 16 **funeral** ceremony during which a dead person is put in a grave or cremated – 18 **preposterous** absurd – 22 **Hibernian** coming from Ireland – **to have s.o. on** to make a joke, to try to make s.o. believe s.th. which is not true – 24 **to bury s.o.** ['berɪ] to put a dead person in a grave – 25 **twerp** *(informal, old-fashioned)* stupid person

American Welcome

Brian Friel*

An hotel lobby. Piped MUSIC in background. Two chairs, one on each side of a small table. On one chair sits the EUROPEAN, a large brown envelope on his lap. HE casually surveys his surroundings. After a few seconds the AMERICAN enters, carrying a briefcase. HE looks around, spots the European, bears down on him. The American is young. HE speaks very rapidly and gives excessive emphasis to several words in each sentence.

AMERICAN. It is Mr. Smith, isn't it? Mr. John Smith? I'd recognize that distinguished head anywhere! I'm Bert – remember? We've corresponded. I'm directing your play. Welcome, sir! Welcome to America!

(THEY shake hands.)

AMERICAN. No-no. Don't get up – please. *(HE sits.)* May I? Well! You've made it! You're here! Gosh! And may I tell you, sir, how honored and how privileged we are to have you here with us.

I'm sure you're still groggy with jet lag, are you? Can I get you something to eat, something to drink? How's your hotel? Had you a good flight? Can I get you a coffee? Tea? Beer? May I call you Joe? Thank you. And may I make a personal comment? You look

* * 1929 in Northern Ireland (Catholic), worked as a teacher before turning to writing plays

1 **piped music** music played on pipes (*Flöten- oder Dudelsackmusik*) – 3 **European** [jʊərə'pi:ən] – **envelope** ['envələʊp] flat paper covering used for sending letters in – **lap** top part of your legs when sitting – **casually** ['kæʒjʊəlɪ] in a relaxed way – 4 **to survey s.th.** [sə'veɪ] to look carefully at every detail of s.th. – 5 **briefcase** a flat case used for carrying papers and documents – 6 **to spot** to see – **to bear down on s.o.** to move quickly towards s.o. in a threatening way – 7 **excessive** extreme – 8 **emphasis** ['emfəsɪs] stress – 10 **distinguished** famous, eminent – 11 **to direct a play** to give the actors and actresses instructions about what they are expected to do on the stage – 15 **gosh** [gɑʃ] (*AE, informal, old-fashioned*) exclamation used to express surprise – 17 **jet lag** feeling of being tired after a long plane journey

so European – it's uncanny! *(Without breaking his speech HE opens his briefcase and takes out a script and a large note-block.)* Wonderful. Okay. Let's get down to business. But before, we do, Jim, may I tell you just once more how magnificent, how truly magnificent your play is – I mean that – and how honored and privileged I am to be associated with it. I really mean that. You see, Bill, what you have given us is a perfectly conceived and perfectly executed analysis of the human condition the world over. It's so perfect it – it – it's frightening. Beautiful form. Electrifying language. Subtle wit. Penetrating insights. I mean to say that's art – that's real art – that's European art, if you know what I mean. What I'm trying to say, Tom, is this: you have entrusted me with this delicate perfection – and I'm scared. I say to myself: Bert, can you handle it? Are you worthy of it?

You're tired. Can I get you something? Coffee? Tea? Beer?

Okay. Fine. What have I got here? A few questions. Do you mind if I ask you a few silly questions? Just for my own enlightenment. I knew you wouldn't mind. And may I tell you, Chuck, how honored and how privileged we are to have you here with us? First problem: language. Frankly we're uneasy with the language. I mean to say we're not uneasy with the language – it's just that there's a lot of it we don't understand. Simply a question of usage: or to be more accurate, simply a question of our ignorance of your usage. I've made a list here – words like "boot," "bumper," "chemist" – there are maybe a dozen of them. Frankly we don't know what you mean. And since you want to communicate with American audiences and since we want them

1 **uncanny** strange – 4 **magnificent** [-'---] excellent – 7 **to conceive** to plan – 8 **to execute** ['---] *here*: to do – 10 **subtle** ['sʌtl] *here:* skilful, clever – **wit** ability to say or write things which are clever and amusing – **penetrating insight** profound understanding – 12 **to entrust s.o. with s.th**. to make it s.o.'s duty to take care of s.th. – 13 **delicate perfection** *here:* carefully composed work – **scared** anxious, filled with fear – 14 **worthy** ['wɜ:ðɪ] – 18 **enlightenment** *here*: deeper understanding – 20 **uneasy with** worried about – 23 **accurate** ['ækjərət] – 24 **ignorance** lack of knowledge – **boot** (*BE*)/**trunk** (*AE*) space at the back of the car where you put bags, etc. – 25 **bumper** (*BE*)/**fender** (*AE*) *Stoßstange* – **chemist** (*BE*)/**druggist** (*AE*) s.o. who prepares and sells medicines in a shop

to understand you, I mean to say what we did was this. We went to our most distinguished American playwright – and you've got to meet him while you're here; he just adores your work – and what he did for us was this. He took all those little confusing words – five or six thousand approximately – and with wonderful delicacy and skill and with the utmost respect for the rhythms and tones of your speech, he did this most beautiful job of translating the play into the language we speak and understand. I hope you'll approve. I know you'll approve.

Can I get you something? Coffee? Tea? Beer? Gosh! I really can't believe it, Mike! You're actually here! I'm just knocked-out!

Okay. Second problem: the form of your play. We're uneasy with the form. I mean to say we're not uneasy with the form – it's just that you've written this wonderful naturalistic play but you've written it in monologue form! A naturalistic play in monologue form, for God's sake! I mean to say a monologue is just not naturalistic if you don't mind my saying so. Let me qualify that instantly. The monologue may be naturalistic in Europe but it is not "natural" to us. We talk, we exchange, we communicate. And since you want to communicate with American audiences and since we want them to understand you, I mean to say what we did was this. We went to our most distinguished American playwright – and you've got to meet him while you're here; he just reveres your work and what he did for us was this. He took your little monologue and with wonderful delicacy and skill and with the utmost respect for the rhythms and tones of your speech, he did this most beautiful job of transforming your script into a four-character, two-act, single-set comedy that is just how can I tell you? – just breathtaking. I hope you'll approve. I know you'll approve.

2 **playwright** s.o. who writes for the theatre – 3 **to adore s.th.** to like s.th. very much – 5 **delicacy** ['delıkəsı] quality of doing s.th. very carefully – 6 **utmost** greatest, most extreme – 8 **to approve** to accept s.th., to think positively about s.th. – 14 **naturalistic** [ˌnætʃərə'lıstık] showing the world as it is – 15 **monologue** ['mɒnəlɒg] – 19 **to exchange** *here*: to express one's own ideas and listen to another person's – 24 **to revere** [rı'vıə] to respect, to admire – 28 **single-set** with a stage showing only one location throughout a play – 29 **breathtaking** ['breθˌteıkıŋ]

You're suffering from jet-lag – I can see it. Can I get you something? Gin? Whisky? Brandy? Gosh! I really can't believe it, Dan! You're actually here! I'm just knocked-out! *(HE sits back, relaxes, smiles contentedly.)* Well, that wasn't too bad now, was it? And here we are, all set to go. And let me tell you this. We think – hell, we know! – that we've got the most distinguished, the funniest, the most sensitive, the most disturbing, the most enlightening and the most moving play of the season – a big, big, big hit that is going to make us all rich and famous.

And may I tell you once more how honored and how privileged we are to have you here with us. May I shake that distinguished hand again?

Welcome, Tony Brown, welcome to America! *(HE takes the European's hand and pumps it with enthusiasm.)*

THE END

4 **contentedly** happily – 5 **to be set to do s.th.** to be prepared to do s.th. – 7 **sensitive** taking people's feelings into account – 8 **enlightening** very successful in describing and making people understand s.th.

Hospital Flash

Courtney Hope

Characters: PATIENT NURSE

PATIENT: Nurse, can I have another glass of water?
NURSE: That's the fifth this afternoon, Number twenty-six.
PATIENT: I can't think of anything else to bring you over here.
NURSE: What nonsense – you can think of several hundred things. You made me shake your pillows up at least ten times yesterday, and the day before you said your dressings were too tight – now it's thirst.
PATIENT: I am thirsty – but not for water.
NURSE: That's all you'll get here.
PATIENT: I'm thirsty for you, Nurse. Has no one told you what you are like?
NURSE: Yes, the Matron – many times.
PATIENT: No. I mean ... what a stunner you are to look at?
NURSE: Lie back, Number twenty-six, and go to sleep ... it's your rest time.
PATIENT: Has no one told you about that dimple inside your elbow?
NURSE: No ... give me the glass back, please. ...
PATIENT: There isn't a girl in France to hold a candle to you.
NURSE: I expect you'd know.
PATIENT: Oh, Nurse, I can't even talk French.
NURSE: I don't suppose that would handicap you either.
PATIENT: If only I could get up. ...
NURSE: Well, You can't. ...
PATIENT: I'd show you how the Tanks make love.

8 **dressing** soft material placed over a wound – 9 **tight** fitting closely (*eng*) – 14 **Matron** ['meɪtrən] (*BE, old-fashioned*) female nurse in charge of the other nurses in a hospital – 15 **stunner** very attractive woman – 18 **dimple** *Grübchen* – 19 **elbow** the middle of your arm, the place where you can bend it – 21 **to (be able to) hold a candle to s.o.** to be as good as s.o. – 27 **Tank** military vehicle covered with steel plates (*Panzer*); *here*: a strong and aggressive person

NURSE: I don't want to be made love to by a Tank.

PATIENT: I mean I'd show you. …

NURSE: I'm quite sure you'd show me a lot, but you happen to be ill and you are now going to rest.

PATIENT: When can I have my pillows shaken up?

NURSE: Are they uncomfortable?

PATIENT: Not half!

NURSE: I don't believe you. You behaved abominably when I shook them yesterday.

PATIENT: Not every time I didn't.

NURSE: I know I was thankful Matron didn't see you.

PATIENT: Scraggy old vinegar bottle. I bet she's never been kissed.

NURSE: I can't discuss the Matron.

PATIENT: My back's all crooked.

NURSE: Then lie straight.

PATIENT: You've no heart. It's as hard as a golf ball.

NURSE: No more talking, Number twenty-six, please.

PATIENT: I've got a temperature. I can feel it rising.

NURSE: I am not listening.

PATIENT: It's because of you. If you'd only hold my hand Nurse dear, it would go down at once.

NURSE: Be quiet.

PATIENT: After all I've been through. …

NURSE: You're only here with appendicitis.

PATIENT: It was all I could get.

NURSE: And now you'll stop talking.

PATIENT: Oh, Nurse, I could just lie here and look at you. I don't want to go away. I don't want to get better.

NURSE: You needn't worry, you won't.

PATIENT *(startled)*: What?

NURSE: You won't get better. The doctor saw you kissing me yesterday, and he happens to be my husband!

Gong!

7 **not half** (*BE, informal*) extremely – 8 **abominable** [ə'bɒmɪnəbl] terrible – 12 **scraggy** too thin – **vinegar** ['vɪnɪgə] *Essig* – 14 **crooked** ['krʊkɪd] bent, not straight – 24 **appendicitis** [əˌpendɪ'saɪtɪs] *Blinddarmentzündung*

On the Pier

Courtney Hope

Characters: HE SHE

SHE: Oh, thank you so much.

HE: Not at all. … I saw you accidentally drop it.

SHE: So good of you … it's my favourite hanky.

HE: It – er – matches your eyes, if you don't mind me saying so.

SHE: Do you really think so? Some people hate blue eyes.

HE: Some people love them.

SHE *(giving him a look)*: Oh!

HE: I've seen you before. … I hope you won't mind me saying this, but I feel I know a lot about you.

SHE: I don't see how you can. I am most frightfully particular. … I *never* talk to strangers as a rule. … I don't know why I am talking to you … you can't be too careful.

HE: No?

SHE: Especially in a seaside place – you do meet such frightful people.

HE: I suppose you do.

SHE: Places *are* so mixed nowadays, you simply don't know who you will have to rub shoulders with.

HE: I know who I should like to.

SHE: Oh, you are ridiculous! No, but, really, I never do talk to people I haven't been introduced to, but of course I can see you are all right.

HE: That's nice of you … don't be angry with me if I say how I admire your dress.

pier ['pɪə] a long structure built in the sea, joined to the land, often containing places of entertainment – 3 **accidentally** [ˌ--'---] not intentionally – 4 **hanky** (*informal*) handkerchief (a piece of paper or cloth for blowing your nose) – 5 **to match (s.th.)** to go together or combine well (with s.th.) – 11/15 **frightful** terrible – 11 **particular** *here*: careful – 19 **to rub shoulders with s.o.** to spend time with s.o.

SHE: *This* old rag? Oh, it's awful. ... I don't think pink suits me.
HE: You ought to wear pale green in the evenings.
SHE: Well! That is odd. I do! I have two pale green evening frocks!
HE: I can just imagine you in them ... and perhaps a pale lemon fluffy one.
SHE: You are marvellous, really. You must be a thought reader.
HE: Well, I told you when I first spoke to you I felt I knew a lot about you.
SHE: I rather feel like that about you, too. I mean I'm an awfully good judge of a person, and, honestly, I'm never wrong.
HE: Does that mean that I'm all right?
SHE: I shouldn't be speaking to you if you weren't.
HE: You staying long?
SHE: A month. ... We came on Saturday. ... We're at the Grand.
HE: Not a bad pub.
SHE: There's a dance there, I believe, to-night.
HE I wish I could – *(Hesitates.)*
SHE *(glancing at him)*: I daresay you could.
HE I'm afraid not.
SHE: Why ever not? People come in from other hotels.
HE: Yes. ... I know you'd be perfect to dance with.
SHE: Oh, I don't know. ... What about trying?
HE: If you only knew how I'd love to.
SHE: Well ... if you come along I could introduce you to the parents. They're rather sticklers.
HE: Oh, yes? They'd want to – er – look me over. I expect they've seen me about. ...
SHE: You live here?
HE: Well – yes ... I'm at the Grand a good bit.
SHE *(laughs)*: There's a good cocktail bar, isn't there?

1 **rag** *here:* a piece of clothing that is worn out – **to suit s.o.** [su:t] to look good on s.o. – 3 **odd** strange – **frock** *(old-fashioned)* dress – 5 **fluffy** soft – 6 **marvellous** ['mɑ:vələs] wonderful – 17 **to hesitate** to stop talking for a moment – 18 **I daresay** a phrase used when you say s.th. that may be true – 20 **Why ever ...?** used in questions expressing surprise – 25 **stickler** s.o. who is very particular about what he/she likes – 29 **a good bit** (*informal*) very often

HE: Rather ...

SHE: I'll have to tell the parents I've been introduced to you ... it's rather awful, only I knew at once that you were one of us – or I'd never have answered you.

HE: Oh, rather.

SHE: Well, drift in to-night. ...

HE: I shall be up there anyhow to-night. Will you wear your lemon frock?

SHE: If you'd like me to.

HE: I love it ... and that big silver bag you carry?

SHE: How – how did you know that? I believe you've been – *spying* on me!

HE: No, but I've noticed all your clothes – and your eyelashes – and the little curl behind this ear.

SHE *(flattered and delighted)*: Well, I have never *seen* you. ...

HE: No, you wouldn't.

SHE: Why, where do you sit?

HE: I don't.

SHE: What – what do you mean?

HE *(after a long pause)*: You have the corner table in the Grand dining-room, madam. I am your waiter!

Black Out.

6 **to drift in** (*informal*) to come in – 10 **to spy on s.o.** (*informal) here*: to collect secret information about s.o. – 13 **eyelashes** (*usu. plural*) the hair growing on the edge of the eyelids – 14 **curl** *Locke* – 15 **to be flattered** to be pleased because s.o. makes you feel important or beautiful – **delighted** filled with joy

There's No Witch at the Hilton

Peg Kehret*

CAST: HUSBAND, WIFE

(The WIFE is sitting, reading or knitting, as the husband enters.)

HUSBAND: Hello … I'm home.

WIFE: Hi.

HUSBAND: Where are the kids?

WIFE: Oh … out.

HUSBAND: Out where?

WIFE: In the woods.

HUSBAND: In the woods? But it's after dark … they'll get lost.

WIFE: That's the idea.

HUSBAND: You didn't!

WIFE: I did.

HUSBAND: I thought we were going to talk about it again tonight.

WIFE: We've talked about it! Every night for two weeks we've talked about it. It was time for action.

HUSBAND: I suppose you're right. I hope you gave them some food.

WIFE: What do you think I am, a wicked stepmother? Of course I gave them some food. Peanut butter and catsup sandwiches.

HUSBAND: Yuck. What kind of thing is that to give them, peanut butter and catsup sandwiches?

WIFE: It's what they like, that's what. Every morning all week long, I have to make peanut butter and catsup sandwiches for their lunches. It's enough to turn my stomach.

HUSBAND: I should think so. They both like that?

* * 1936 in the USA, lives in Washington State, published plays and short stories, then took to writing books for children, won several awards

18 **wicked** ['wɪkɪd] evil, very bad – **stepmother** a woman married to your father who is not your natural mother – 19 **catsup** (*AE*) ketchup – 20 **yuck** (*informal*) exclamation expressing dislike or disgust

WIFE: Hansel wants mustard on his, too, but I draw the line at that.

HUSBAND: How long ago did you take them?

WIFE: Oh, a couple of hours. Will you stop worrying? They'll get along OK. It's probably the woods we should worry about. With Hansel on the loose, it's liable to be an ecological disaster out there.

HUSBAND: It sure seems quiet around here.

WIFE: Do you want to go to a movie?

HUSBAND: Can we get a sitter this late?

WIFE: What do we need with a sitter?

HUSBAND: That's right. Say, maybe there will be advantages to this arrangement.

WIFE: I knew you'd like it.

HUSBAND: I didn't say that. It's going to be very lonesome without my little Gretel here to –

WIFE: Spill her milk at the dinner table.

HUSBAND: I was going to say, without my Gretel here to –

WIFE: Wet the bed every night.

HUSBAND: Will you stop that?

WIFE: Well, it's true. How does she manage that, do you suppose?

HUSBAND: Manage what?

WIFE: To spill every liquid she gets and still he able to wet the bed.

HUSBAND: You aren't being fair. Lots of kids wet their beds.

WIFE: 'Til they're fourteen?

HUSBAND: She isn't fourteen and you know it.

WIFE: Well, I'd be willing to bet my last nickel that when she is fourteen, she'll still be doing it.

HUSBAND: Speaking of last nickels, can we afford to go to a movie tonight? I'm broke.

1 **mustard** spicy sauce (*Senf*) – **to draw the line at s.th.** *here:* not to do s.th. – 3 **to take s.o. somewhere** to go somewhere with s.o. – 6 **with … on the loose** [lu:s] with … being free – **liable** ['laɪəbl] likely, probable – 10 **sitter** babysitter – 15 **lonesome** ['ləʊnsəm] lonely – 17 **to spill** to make liquids flow over the edge of a cup, etc. – 23 **liquid** a substance that flows – 27 **to bet one's last nickel** *(fig.)* to be very sure of s.th. – 30 **broke** (*informal*) having no money

WIFE: We can put it on our credit card.

HUSBAND: Good thinking. What's playing, anyway?

WIFE: "Goldilocks and the Bare Three."

HUSBAND: But that's rated X.

WIFE: Good. It's about time we saw an X film. I'm sick of Walt Disney.

HUSBAND: I guess there's no reason we can't go, as long as we aren't taking the kids.

WIFE: Hansel would probably have loved it.

HUSBAND: What's that supposed to mean?

WIFE: I caught him reading *Playboy* again last night.

HUSBAND: So he's a normal red-blooded boy, with a little curiosity. Lots of kids buy *Playboy.*

WIFE: The Braille issue?

HUSBAND: I didn't even know it came that way. Must be some center fold-out!

WIFE: Not only that, his teacher called again.

HUSBAND: What did she want this time?

WIFE: It seems Hansel had a profitable little business going in the cafeteria. He charged the other children a penny each for the paper napkins.

HUSBAND: That doesn't seem so high.

WIFE: The napkins were furnished free by the school.

HUSBAND: Oh. Well, at least that's better than the time he tape-recorded our discussion about your mother and then played it for Show-and-Tell.

3 ***Goldilocks and the Three Bears*** [beəz] an English fairy story; here turned into a pun (play on words): bare [beə] = naked – 4 **an X-rated film** a film with graphic sexual content which people under 18 are not allowed to see – 12 **red-blooded** full of strength or sexual energy – **curiosity** [ˌkjʊərɪ'ɒsətɪ] strong desire to know about s.th. – 14 **Braille issue** ['breɪl ˌɪʃu:] edition with a system of printing which the blind can read – 16 **center fold-out** (*AE*) picture of an (almost) naked woman, forming the middle pages of a magazine – 19 **profitable** ['----] money-making – 21 **napkin** a piece of paper or cloth used to wipe your mouth, etc. at meals – 23 **to furnish** to provide – 26 ***Show-and-Tell*** an activity where a student shows s.th. to other students and talks about it

WIFE: Discussion? You called my mother a frustrated old hen, who needed a good rooster, and that kid played it for the whole world.

HUSBAND: It was not the whole world. Only the fifth grade class.

WIFE: Judging from the phone calls I got the next day, there must have been four hundred and fifty kids in that fifth grade class.

HUSBAND: I already apologized for that, so let's not get into it again. Your mother's gone now anyway, God rest her soul.

WIFE: Probably died of embarrassment to have such a grandson.

HUSBAND: She's the one who gave him that tape recorder. Besides, all you talk about are the bad times. We had some good times with the kids, too.

WIFE: Name one.

HUSBAND: Our vacation was fun last year.

WIFE: Especially when Gretel spilled her milk in the restaurant and wet the motel bed.

HUSBAND: Well, what about little league? You have to admit you like going to the little league games.

WIFE: Yes. Yes, I did like the little league. But you're forgetting that letter we got from the coach at the end of the season asking us not to sign Hansel up again next year.

HUSBAND: Oh, yes, that little business about him doing a hair oil commercial in his little league uniform.

WIFE: He should have known that would lose him his amateur standing.

HUSBAND: So he made a mistake. He's only a kid.

WIFE: One mistake I could overlook. One an hour, no.

HUSBAND: OK, OK Lets not argue anymore. We'll be late for the movie.

2 **rooster** cock – 4 **fifth grade** *(AE)* fifth year (at school) – 8 **God rest her soul** said when you are talking about a dead person; soul = the immortal spirit of a person – 9 **embarrassment** [ɪm'bærəsmənt] feeling of guilt or shame (*Verlegenheit*) – 16 **wet** *past tense of* to wet, *also* wetted – 17 **little league** [li:g] a group of baseball teams for players ages 8–12 – 20 **coach** *Trainer(in)* – 21 **to sign s.o. up** *jdn. anmelden* – 23 **commercial** [kə'mɜ:ʃl] advert, e.g. on TV or in the press – 24 **amateur standing** ['æmətə ˌ--] the status of an amateur

WIFE: I just have to fix my hair. *(She gets her purse, opens it and starts to rummage through.)* My credit cards. I can't find my credit cards! *(She digs furiously in her purse, then dumps it upside down. The only contents are: a comb, lipstick, pencil, handkerchief and a piece of paper.)* They're gone! Someone stole all my credit cards!

HUSBAND: Are you sure? *(He starts to look through the articles that fell from the purse. He picks up the piece of paper.)* What's this? It looks like a letter.

WIFE: I don't know. What does it say?

HUSBAND: It's from Hansel! *(He reads.)* "Dear Stepmother, We heard you are planning to leave us in the woods, so we've taken all your credit cards, to make sure we have enough to eat and a place to stay. If you change your minds and want us back, you can contact us at the Forest Hilton."

WIFE: The Forest Hilton? What kind of money does he think a woodchopper makes?

HUSBAND: Pretty good taste, for a kid his age. We've never even stayed there.

WIFE: You won't think it's so smart when you get the bill.

HUSBAND: I wonder if room service has peanut butter and catsup sandwiches.

WIFE: If they didn't before, I'll bet they do now.

HUSBAND: What shall we do?

WIFE: We can't leave them there, running up a big bill.

HUSBAND: Maybe if we try living on less money …

WIFE: While they stay at the Forest Hilton? No way!

HUSBAND: If I declare bankruptcy, we wouldn't have to pay any of the bills.

WIFE: But they'd make us take the kids back.

HUSBAND: True.

2 **to rummage** ['rʌmɪdʒ] to move things around because you want to find s.th. – 3 **to dig** *here:* to search for s.th. – **to dump s.th.** to empty a container, bag, etc. out quickly – 4 **comb** [kəʊm] flat piece of plastic used to make your hair neat – 5 **handkerchief** ['hæŋkətʃɪːf] a piece of paper or cloth for blowing your nose – 17 **woodchopper** s.o. who cuts wood into pieces – 25 **to run up a bill** to allow a bill to become high – 27 **No way!** Absolutely not! – 28 **bankruptcy** ['bæŋkrəptsɪ] inability to pay one's debts

WIFE: Maybe we could report them as runaways and they'd get sent to juvenile court and put in a foster home.

HUSBAND: Wait a minute. There's a P.S. on this note. *(He reads.)* "In case you have any ideas about not taking us back, you should know that I made a tape recording of you when you were discussing how to get rid of us. No doubt the police would find it very interesting if it was mailed to them after we disappear." *(He looks up.)* I told your mother not to give him that tape recorder.

WIFE: Well, it's too late now. What are we going to do?

HUSBAND: What choice do we have?

WIFE: We'll have to go get the kids and bring them home.

HUSBAND: Right. Come on, we might as well get it over with.

WIFE: By the time I get to an X-rated movie, I'll be too old to care.

(They exit.)

2 **juvenile court** ['dʒu:vənaɪl 'kɔ:t] law court which deals with young offenders or criminals – **foster home** a home where a child is taken care of by people who are not his/her parents – 3 **P.S.** *short for* postscript, a note written at the end of a letter – 6 **to get rid of s.o.** to free oneself of s.o. who is unwanted – 13 **to get s.th. over with** to complete s.th. unpleasant

Honest Abe – Can He Stay That Way?

Bill Majeski

CAST: ANNOUNCER, male or female, On-Stage or Off; ABE Lincoln; MANNIE, his White House aide and political advisor. He is glib, sure of himself.

SETTING: Table or desk with two chairs.

(OPENING: Both men are On-Stage. ABE is seated, holding paper and pencil. MANNIE is seated.)

ANNOUNCER: Throughout the history of our country, our presidents have had speech writers and advisors who suggest ways in which the leaders can grab more votes and, more importantly, not offend any particular group. One president, considered by many to be the finest writer in White House history, did his own work. But could he withstand today's pressures brought about by powerful blocs of voters? Let's take a look as we see this president, Abraham Lincoln, going over a speech with his advisor, Mannie.

MANNIE: OK, Abe, lay it on me.

ARE: Fourscore and seven years ago our fathers brought …

MANNIE: Hold it right there, Abe, Fathers? You just can't say fathers. Mothers were involved here too.

ABE: I know, but …

MANNIE: Do you realize the clout these women's groups have?

ABE: Women's groups?

MANNIE: They're all over the place. You've got your WAWA's, your …

ABE: *(Puzzled)* WAWA's?

MANNIE: Wide Awake Women of America. You've got MAN …

2 **aide** [eɪd] person whose job it is to help others – 3 **glib** fast-talking – 9 **to grab** *here*: to get – 12 **to withstand** to resist – 13 **bloc** group – 16 **to lay s.th. on s.o.** (*informal*) *here*: to tell s.o. one's ideas – 17 **fourscore** *(old use)* eighty (four times twenty) – 21 **clout** power and influence

ARE: *(Interrupting)* Man? Thought you said women's groups.

MANNIE: It is a women's group ... a mean, militant mob. MAN is the acronym for Mean and Nasty.

ABE: Look, Mannie ...

MANNIE: You've got the DAR.

ABE: The Daughters I know.

MANNIE: There's the WASHUS, the ...

ABE: Washus? The Indians have always liked me ...

MANNIE: Not Indians, Abe. Women. WASHUS stands for Women Against Sexual Harassment from Union Soldiers.

ARE: Sexual harassment by soldiers? Never. At least no Union soldiers.

MANNIE: Well, I've seen some of them and I can't believe anybody would want to harass them. I'm with you on that one, Abe, but they're a force you have to consider.

ABE: OK, I'm considering.

MANNIE: Let's go back. Instead of fathers ... substitute parents.

ARE: *(Checking speech)* Hmm ... fourscore and seven years ago our parents brought forth ... I don't know ... doesn't have the same zing.

MANNIE: Zing, schming, it don't mean a thing if you ain't got that swing with the female voters.

ABE: *(Reluctantly)* Gee, I don't know ...

MANNIE: You can't say fathers.

ABE: What about freedom of speech, the first amendment?

MANNIE: Hey, you can't hide behind the constitution. You're the president.

ABE: I'm a citizen and I'm entitled to my civil rights.

2 **mob** *(informal)* a large, unmannerly, chaotic group – 3 **acronym** ['ækrənɪm] word formed from the first letters of a sequence of words, e.g. *Unicef, Aids* – 10 **harassment** ['hærəsmənt] unpleasant, offensive comments and actions – 15 **to consider s.th.** to think about s.th. carefully – 17 **to substitute** ['---] to use s.th. else instead – 19 **to bring forth** (*old use, formal*) to produce – 20 **zing** (*informal*) appeal, attraction – 21 **schming** *invented onomatopoetic expression, rhyming with* zing – 22 **swing** (*informal*) *here:* popularity – 23 **gee** [dʒi:] exclamation expressing surprise – 25 **amendment** [-'--] a change of or addition to a formal document, decision, etc. (*here:* the American constitution) – 28 **to be entitled to s.th.** to have a right to s.th.

MANNIE: Civil rights? You ain't no minority.

ARE: No minority? How many guys do you know that are six-feet-four, have a beard and wear a stovepipe hat?

MANNIE: Yeah, I want to talk to you about that hat later. But let's get back to your little talk here.

ABE: *(Irritated, hands the speech over to MANNIE.)* Here, you read it. *(MANNIE takes paper.)*

MANNIE: Yeah, I'll have a look-see. Maybe I can punch it up.

ABE: *(Stands, talks story-telling style.)* A fellow came up to me the other day and asked, "Mr. President, how long should a man's legs be?"

MANNIE: *(Looking up)* "Just long enough to reach the ground." Hey, we heard it. Don't run it into the ground. Let me finish this.

ABE: *(Chastened, sits back down.)* OK, OK.

MANNIE: Not bad, not bad. I go along with all this until we get to this – *(Reads aloud)* "that this nation, under God ..." Abe. *(Shakes head.)* Abey baby. What are you doing to me? You can't say "under God."

ABE: And why not?

MANNIE: Do you realize how many God-fearing atheists and agnostics you got out there?

ABE: Isn't that an oxymoron or am I missing something?

MANNIE: I don't care how intelligent they are. They vote, that's all I know.

ABE: And I want "under God" in there, that's all I know.

MANNIE: Look, these people are tough. They got groups. And believe me, these atheists got lots of friends in Congress.

ABE: *That* I can believe.

MANNIE: I mean you've got your ALAB – Atheists Living and Breathing. The Triple A, Agnostic Atheist Association ... see,

3 **stovepipe hat** an old-fashioned hat having the shape of a stovepipe (*Ofenrohr*) that Lincoln often wore – 8 **to punch s.th. up** (*informal*) to make s.th. better, to improve s.th. – 13 **to run s.th. into the ground** to say s.th. so often that it does not have any effect any longer – 14 **chastened** ['tʃeɪsnd] realizing that one has made a mistake – 20 **atheist** ['eɪθiɪst] person who believes that there is no God – **agnostic** [æg'nɒstɪk] person who believes we cannot know if God exists – 22 **oxymoron** [ˌɒksɪ'mɔːrɒn] a combination of two opposite words, e.g. *cruel kindness* – **to miss s.th.** not to understand s.th.

they'll combine to gang up on you. And one of the biggest – the Atheists Society In the Northern Interior and the New Earth – or ASININE.

ABE: You got *that* right.

MANNIE: You can't hurt atheists, Abe. Once they pull that curtain shut in the booth, they vote with their hearts and souls.

ABE: Let me tell you a little story …

MANNIE: This isn't going to be one of those aphorisms like the one about McClellan having his headquarters where his hindquarters should be?

ABE: *(Going right on)* This atheist died and he's lying there in his coffin. And my Aunt Polly said: "Look at him. All dressed up and no place to go."

MANNIE: Yeah, right Abe. Tell Aunt Polly she gets a three on the laugh meter.

ABE: I like "under God." And it'll catch on. I bet someday we'll have a saying something like "in God we trust" on all our money.

MANNIE: Yeah. And the moon is made of green liederkranz and it don't rain in Indianapolis in the summertime. *(MANNIE hands the paper back.)* Here, make those two changes. *(ABE refuses, stands up.)*

ABE: Keep it. Print it. It stands as it is. No president should ever succumb to the pressures of the power-seeking, self-serving organizations, no matter what kind. This is a government "of the

1 **to combine** to come together in order to work together – **to gang up on s.o.** (*informal*) to form a group to attack, hurt or frighten s.o. – 6 **booth** [bu:ð] cabin in which a person can do s.th. privately (*here*: vote) – 8 **aphorism** ['æfərɪzm] a short phrase which says s.th. wise – 9 **McClellan** [mə'klelən] general of the Northern Union during the American Civil War (1861–65), who was unsuccessful as a military commander – 10 **hindquarters** ['haɪnd͵kwɔ:təz] back part of a four-legged animal – 12 **coffin** box for a dead person – **dressed up** wearing very elegant or formal clothes – 14 **a three** three points out of ten – 15 **meter** device to measure s.th. – 16 **to catch on** to become popular – 19 **liederkranz** ['li:də͵kræns] strong-flavoured soft cheese – 24 **to succumb to s.th.** [sə'kʌm] to give in to s.th.

people, by the people, for the people" – read that – *(Gesturing to paper)* it's in there. That means all the people, not big lobbies and angry mobs. (*ABE exits.)*

MANNIE: *(Resigned to defeat, shrugs and glances at paper. Murmurs as be reads.)* Gettysburg address. Address? *(Calls after ABE.)* Abe, call this an address? You ain't got no street or number! *(Shouts even louder.)* And you forgot the zip code! *(Starts after ABE, then returns and sits down, shakes head.)* I don't know what I'm gonna do with that boy.

1 **to gesture to s.th.** ['dʒestʃə] to point at s.th. – 2 **lobby** pressure group – 4 **resigned to defeat** accepting calmly that one has lost – **to shrug** to raise your shoulders to show that you do not know or care about s.th. – **to glance at s.th.** to look quickly at s.th. – 5 **to murmur** to say s.th. in a quiet voice that is difficult to understand – ***Gettysburg address*** [ˌgetɪsbɜːg əˈdres] famous speech (or address) given by Lincoln in 1863, i.e. in the middle of the American Civil War (1861–65) – **address** *play on words:* either a speech or house number, etc. describing where s.o. lives – 7 **zip code** (AE) postcode

The Subway Werewolf

Richard Mauro

CAST: WEREWOLF (Dressed normally, no werewolf makeup); PASSENGERS 1, 2, 3.

SETTING: Chairs can be set up to form a bench on a subway train.

WEREWOLF: *(Howls like werewolf)* Ahooooooooo! *(PASSENGERS 1–3 move away from WEREWOLF, who tries to scare them with another howl.)* Ahhoooooooo! *(Looks at PASSENGERS, who now try not to laugh.)* Well ... aren't you afraid? Terrified? *(To PASSENGER 1's face)* What about you?

PASSENGER 1: *(Trying not to laugh or show fear)* N-not really.

WEREWOLF: Oh. I get it. You probably see a lot of weird people like me who howl on the subway at midnight when the moon is full. Is that it? *(To PASSENGER 2)* Is that it? Well? Is it?

PASSENGER 2: You'd be surprised what you see on the subway at midnight. Some howl, some mumble, some tap dance.

WEREWOLF: No kidding. Really?

PASSENGER 3: Oh, yes. It happens all the time, especially at midnight when the moon is full. I guess the subway just has a way of attracting ... er –

WEREWOLF: Weirdos? Crazies? Nuts? Loonies?

PASSENGER 1: Right. It's this city. I guess with all the hustle and bustle of a job, a decent place to live, or just getting from one

subway (*AE*)/**underground** (*BE*) – **werewolf** ['weəwʊlf] character in fairy stories and fables who sometimes changes into a wolf (especially at the time of the full moon) – 4 **to howl** [haʊl] to make long loud cries (like a wolf, dog, etc.) – 10 **weird** [wɪəd] very unusual or strange – 14 **to mumble** to say s.th. with a quiet voice in an unclear manner – **to tap dance** to dance wearing shoes with metal pieces (*Stepp tanzen*) – 15 **no kidding** expression used to stress or express surprise that s.th. is true – 19 **weirdo** ['wiədəʊ] *(informal)* person who looks strange – **nuts, loonies** *(informal)* crazy people – 20 **hustle and bustle** [ˌhʌsl ən 'bʌsl] very hectic activity place to another on this crazy subway, it's inevitable that a few people just go … er –

WEREWOLF: Bonkers? Bananas? Is that what you think? You think I howl because I'm crazy?

PASSENGERS 1–3: Welllll.

WEREWOLF: No, no, no. That's not it at all. Can't you see? Look at me. *(PASSENGERS look at WEREWOLF)* See? Isn't it obvious? *(To PASSENGER 3)* Don't you see what I am?

PASSENGER 3: Um, you're an actor? And we're on Kandid Kamera? *(WEREWOLF shakes his head no.)* A brain surgeon? *(WEREWOLF shakes his head no.)* A rocket scientist?

WEREWOLF: *(Screams so loud PASSENGERS 1–3 jump.)* Nooooo! I'm a werewolf.

PASSENGERS 1–3: A werewolf?!

WEREWOLF: Yes! Geez! You'd think it was obvious! Can't you see my hairy face? My fangs? *(To PASSENGER 2)* Well? Can't you see I'm a werewolf?

PASSENGER 2: *(Scared)* Er … well … you look normal.

WEREWOLF: Normal?! I'm a raging werewolf.

PASSENGER 3: Look, buddy. I'm a psychiatrist –

WEREWOLF: Well, woop-tee-doo. A psychiatrist. I suppose you're going to say I'm suffering from some far-out delusion. Right?

PASSENGER 3: Exactly. You see, you've probably been under a lot of stress. Maybe you're a stockbroker, or a computer programmer –

PASSENGERS 1 and 2: Or a subway passenger.

1 **inevitable** [ɪ'nevɪtəbl] not to be avoided – 3 **bonkers, bananas** completely mad or crazy – 7 **obvious** clear – 9 **Kandid Kamera** *normal spelling Candid Camera*, TV programme similar to *Versteckte Kamera* – 10 **brain surgeon** ['sɜːdʒn] doctor who operates on people's brains – 15 **geez** [dʒiːz] exclamation expressing surprise or irritation – 16 **fangs** the two long sharp front teeth in the mouth of some animals (e.g. dogs) – 19 **raging** acting extremely angrily – 20 **buddy** (*informal*) friend – **psychiatrist** [saɪ'kaɪətrɪst] – 21 **woop-tee-doo** an exclamation meaning "So what! Who cares!" – 22 **far-out delusion** very unlikely, unreasonable idea about s.th. – 25 **stockbroker** *Börsenmakler*

PASSENGER 3: Er ... whatever. Anyhow, you've obviously been under a lot of pressure and you only *think* you're a werewolf. It's a way of taking a, shall we say, vacation from reality – from the stress of your true identity and high-pressure life.

WEREWOLF: I knew it! I knew I wasn't a werewolf.

PASSENGERS 1 and 2: *(To PASSENGER 3)* Great work, doc! You cured him!

WEREWOLF: I'm cured! I knew I wasn't a werewolf. *(Stands up and begins to walk and act like a robot.)* I'm an android from Mars! *(PASSENGERS hide behind newspapers.)*

7 **to cure** to heal

Devil of an Interview

Daron Scott McFarland*

CAST: LOIS (may also be LOUIS), SATAN (I'm not sure of the gender, to be honest)
SETTING: Office
PROPS: Phone

LOIS: *(On phone)* Hello, Ms. Miller. Send in Ms. Furr. *(SATAN enters.)* Ah, yes, Ms. Furr. Oh, I'm sorry I was expecting a Lucy Furr.

SATAN: That would be me. But you may call me Satan.

LOIS: *(Writing on SATAN's application)* Prefers to be called Satan.

SATAN: No. I prefer being called, "Oh, Great Dark Master." But Satan will do in a pinch.

LOIS: Please, have a seat. And I take it you're here for the customer service job.

SATAN: *(Sitting)* Yes.

LOIS: Are you currently employed?

SATAN: Self-employed, yes. I'm a talent scout of sorts. I'm in human resources, you might say.

LOIS: I see.

SATAN: But my heart has always been in working within the customer service field.

LOIS: What exactly do you do at your current job?

* Works as an actor, writer, stuntman, director and producer; lives in California

1 **Satan** ['seɪtən] – 2 **gender** [dʒ] sex (male or female) – 5 **Ms.** [mɪz] a title that leaves open whether you are addressing an unmarried (Miss) or married (Mrs) woman – 9 **application** *here*: a form one fills in to apply for a job – 12 **in a pinch** in a difficult situation – 13 **to take it** to assume or suppose – 16 **currently** at the present time – 17 **self-employed** not employed by a company, working for oneself – **talent scout** a person whose job is to find persons who are good at s.th. – **of sorts** (*informal*) in a way, sort of – 18 **resources** [rɪ'zɔːsɪz] *here:* people's skills and abilities

SATAN: I mercilessly torture lost souls with the utmost cruelty.

LOIS: Oh, so you work at the DMV. May I ask you why you wish to leave your current job?

SATAN: It's not as fun as it used to be. All I do is meet the same type of grouchy, yelling, screaming, swearing souls day in and day out. So I figure I need a change of pace.

LOIS: I'm not sure you'll find it in customer service.

SATAN: I also wanted something with vacation time and a retirement package. Besides, if you can't take the heat, get out of the kitchen, so to speak.

LOIS: You have your residence listed as Hades.

SATAN: It's a terrible commute.

LOIS: You seem to have some very interesting references listed here. The problem is that they're all dead. Over a hundred years dead.

SATAN: That isn't a problem, is it?

LOIS: Well, it does make things a bit more difficult. Have you ever attended college?

SATAN: Oh, yes. Many times.

LOIS: Which one?

SATAN: All of them.

LOIS: All of them? Sir, there are several hundred universities and colleges. And you attended all of them?

SATAN: Correct.

LOIS: Then which one did you attend most recently?

1 **merciless** showing no kindness or pity – **to torture s.o.** ['tɔ:tʃə] to hurt s.o. in a cruel way – **soul** the immortal spirit of a person – **utmost** most extreme – 2 **DMV** in the US the abbreviation of Department or Division of Motor Vehicles (*Straßenverkehrsamt*) – 5 **grouchy** (*informal*) bad-tempered and complaining – **to yell** to shout loudly – **to swear** [sweə] to use impolite language – 6 **to figure** *here*: to think – **a change of pace** s.th. different – 8 **retirement package** arrangement for receiving money when you are too old to work (old-age or retirement pension) – 9–10 **if you can't take the heat, get out of the kitchen** *(fig.)* if you can't deal with a difficult situation, you need to get out of it – 11 **residence** ['rezɪdəns] the place where you live – **Hades** ['heɪdi:z] land of the dead (in ancient Greek stories) – 12 **commute** [kə'mju:t] (*esp. AE*) the daily journey to one's workplace – 13 **reference** ['refərəns] a person who can give information about your character and abilities to a new employer – 25 **recently** not long ago

SATAN: Oh, I'm spending a great deal of time at UCLA nowadays. I used to raise hell at NYU. But the last school I was at would have to have been in Oxford.

LOIS: You went to school in Oxford?

SATAN: Yes. Oxford, Mississippi.

LOIS: Oh. Old Miss. Well, let me just pull your transcripts up on the computer.

SATAN: Why?

LOIS: So I can find out your history. It'll only take a few seconds. *(LOIS types on the keyboard.)*

SATAN: *(Looking skyward)* Pssst. St. Peter. You getting a load of this? Why don't you do us both a favor and innovate, you slowpoke?

LOIS: I can't seem to find anything on the computer pertaining to you at the University of Mississippi under the name of Satan or Lucy Furr. Did you attend under the guise of another alias?

SATAN: Try Old Scratch. *(LOIS tries.)*

LOIS: Sorry. Nothing there.

SATAN. Try Devil.

LOIS No dice.

SATAN: Mephisto.

LOIS: Nada.

SATAN: Beelzebub.

LOIS: There is a Belza Bubba.

SATAN: That was me! Bubba! Yep. My college nickname.

LOIS: It says here that Bubba died three years ago.

SATAN: Oh. Well, I got better.

LOIS: Are you married?

1 **UCLA** University of California/Los Angeles – 2 **to raise hell** (*informal)* to cause a lot of trouble – **NYU** New York University – 6 **transcript** ['--] a copy of one's school or university record – 11 **to get a load of s.th.** (*informal*) to look at or listen to s.th. – 12 **to do s.o. a favor** *(AE, BE:* favour) to do s.th. to help s.o. – **to innovate** *here:* to think up s.th. new to do – **slowpoke** (*informal*) a person who acts too slowly – 14 **to pertain to s.th.** [pə'teɪn] to be connected with s.th. – 16 **under the guise** [gaɪz] **of another alias** ['eɪlɪəs] using another name – 20 **no dice** (*informal*) *here:* nothing – 22 **nada** (*Spanish*) nothing – 23 **Beelzebub** [biː'elzɪbʌb] - 25 **yep** (*informal*) yes

SATAN: Nothing you can prove.

LOIS: Look, Mr. Furr, I don't think you'll work out here.

SATAN: Oh, me damn it! *(LOIS looks up at SATAN. SATAN looks back at LOIS.)* Sorry. I have a superiority complex. Come on. Just give me a chance. Please. Please. Oh, pretty please. I'll change my ways. I'll live a good life. I'll go to church every day. Please.

LOIS: OK. OK. I didn't realize it meant that much to you.

SATAN: Just repeating pleadings I've heard. It's the first it ever worked though.

LOIS: *(Picks up phone.)* Ms. Miller, have customer service route their next call into my office. Thank you. *(Hangs up.)* OK, Satan. The next call coming in will be a customer calling with questions, complaints, etc. We'll see how you handle it and I'll make my determination on your possible employment here on it. *(The phone rings. LOIS nods and SATAN answers the phone.)*

SATAN: Hello, Jonathan. Of course I know it's you. And don't think you're going to try to return that radio for a refund. It wasn't faulty. I know you dropped it down the stairs. Of course I know it! And I know you keep those nudie magazines in the toolshed so your wife won't find them. Right under the cigarettes you said you'd give up. If your wife wasn't so dependent on the workers comp you're getting from that back injury you've been faking she would have left you for the shipping manager who just so happens to work at our competitor's store. Have a nice day. *(Hangs up.)* So, how'd I do?

1 **to prove** [u:] to show that s.th. is true – 4 **superiority complex** the opposite of inferiority complex – 9 **pleading** act of begging for s.th. – 11 **to have s.o. do s.th.** to arrange that s.o. does s.th. – **to route** [ru:t] to direct – 15 **determination** *here*: decision – 19 **refund** ['ri:fʌnd] sum of money paid back to you because you returned goods – 20 **faulty** not working or not made correctly – 21 **nudie magazine** (*informal*) magazine with pictures of naked women – 22 **toolshed** small simple building usually of wood where you keep your tools (e.g. hammers, screwdrivers etc.) – 24 **comp** (*informal abbreviation*) compensation – 25 **to fake** to make s.th. false appear genuine or true – **shipping manager** person in a company whose job it is to post goods to customers – 26 **competitor** [-'---] company or person that is your rival (*Konkurrent*)

LOIS: *(Flabbergasted)* All I can say is, "Welcome aboard" to our new customer service manager. *(LOIS shakes SATAN's hand. Both rise and LOIS walks SATAN to the door.)* That was impressive. I may even be able to move you up to collections.
SATAN: I do have some experience in that area.
LOIS: Really? *(Curtain/Blackout)*

1 **flabbergasted** extremely surprised – 4 **collections** department which collects money from customers who do not pay

Applicant

Harold Pinter *

An office, LAMB, a young man, eager, cheerful, enthusiastic, is striding nervously, alone. The door opens. MISS PIFFS comes in. She is the essence of efficiency.

PIFFS: Ah, good morning.

LAMB: Oh, good morning, miss.

PIFFS: Are you Mr. Lamb?

LAMB: That's right.

PIFFS *[studying a sheet of paper]*: Yes, You're applying for this vacant post, aren't you?

LAMB: I am actually, yes.

PIFFS: Are you a physicist?

LAMB: Oh yes, indeed. It's my whole life.

PIFFS *[languidly]*: Good. Now our procedure is, that before we discuss the applicant's qualifications we like to subject him to a little test to determine his psychological suitability. You've no objection?

LAMB: Oh, good heavens, no.

PIFFS: Jolly good.

MISS PIFFS has taken some objects out of a drawer and goes to LAMB. She places a chair for him.

* * 1930 in London where he still lives and works; one of the most successful 20th century British playwrights; writes for the theatre (*The Birthday Party, The Caretaker*), for the screen (*Handmaid's Tale*) and for the radio; received numerous rewards

applicant ['æplɪkənt] person who applies for a job – 1 **eager** interested and excited – **cheerful** happy – 2 **to stride** to walk with long steps – 3 **the essence of s.th.** ['esns] *here:* a perfect example of s.th. – **efficiency** [i'fɪʃnsɪ] the quality of working effectively – 9 **vacant post** ['veɪkənt] job which is available for s.o. to take – 13 **languid** slow, without enthusiasm – **procedure** [prə'si:dʒə] – 14 **to subject s.o. to s.th.** [səb'dʒekt] to make s.o. undergo or experience s.th. – 15 **to determine s.th.** to decide on s.th. – 16 **objection** a reason why you are opposed to s.th. – 18 **jolly good** (*informal*) very good – 19 **drawer** [drɔ:] box with a handle which can be pulled out from a desk or cupboard

PIFFS: Please sit down. *[He sits.]* Can I fit these to your palms?
LAMB *[affably]*: What are they?
PIFFS: Electrodes.
LAMB: Oh yes, of course. Funny little things.

She attaches them to his palms.

PIFFS: Now the earphones.

She attaches earphones to his head.

LAMB: I say how amusing.
PIFFS: Now I plug in.

She plugs in to the wall.

LAMB *[a trifle nervously]*: Plug in, do you? Oh yes, of course. Yes, you'd have to, wouldn't you?

MISS PIFFS perches on a high stool and looks down on LAMB.

This help to determine my ... my suitability does it?
PIFFS: Unquestionably. Now relax. Just relax. Don't think about a thing.
LAMB: No.
PIFFS: Relax completely. Rela-a-a-x. Quite relaxed?

LAMB nods. MISS PIFFS presses a button on the side of her stool. A piercing high pitched buzz-hum is heard. LAMB jolts rigid. His hands go to his earphones. He is propelled from the chair. He tries to crawl under the chair. MISS PIFFS watches, impassive. The noise stops. LAMB peeps out from under the

1 **palm** [pɑ:m] inner surface of the hand – 2 **affable** ['æfəbl] pleasant, friendly – 3 **electrode** [ɪ'lektrəʊd - 6 **earphones** headphones *(Kopfhörer)* – 26 **to plug in** to connect an electrical appliance to a socket – 11 **a trifle** ['traɪfl] slightly, a little – 13 **to perch** to sit on the edge of s.th. – 20 **piercing** (of sounds) very intense (*durchdringend*) – **high pitched** (of sounds) very high – **buzz-hum** continuous sound like that of a bee – **to jolt** [dʒəʊlt] to move suddenly – 21 **rigid** ['rɪdʒɪd] stiff – **to propel** [prə'pel] to push forward in a particular direction – 23 **impassive** not showing any feeling – **to peep** to look secretly

chair, crawls out, stands, switches, emits a short chuckle and collapses in the chair.

PIFFS: Would you say you were an excitable person?

LAMB: Not – not unduly, no. Of course, I –

PIFFS: Would you say you were a moody person?

LAMB: Moody? No, I wouldn't say I was moody – well, sometimes occasionally I –

PIFFS: Do you ever get fits of depression?

LAMB: Well, I wouldn't call them depression exactly –

PIFFS: Do you often do things you regret in the morning?

LAMB: Regret? Things I regret? Well, it depends what you mean by often, really – I mean when you say often –

PIFFS: Are you often puzzled by women?

LAMB: Women?

PIFFS: Men.

LAMB: Men? Well, I was just going to answer the question about women –

PIFFS: Do you often feel puzzled?

LAMB: Puzzled?

PIFFS: By women.

LAMB: Women?

PIFFS: Men.

LAMB: Oh, now just a minute, I ... Look, do you want separate answers or a joint answer?

PIFFS: After your day's work do you ever feel tired? Edgy? Fretty? Irritable? At a loose end? Morose? Frustrated? Morbid? Unable to concentrate? Unable to sleep? Unable to eat? Unable to remain seated? Unable to remain upright? Lustful? Indolent?

1 **to switch** to change one's position – **to emit** [ɪ'mɪt] **a chuckle** to let out a quiet laugh – 3 **excitable** easily excited – 4 **unduly** (*formal*) more than is normal – 5 **moody** often bad-tempered or upset – 8 **fit** sudden attack – 10 **to regret s.th.** to feel sorry about s.th. – 13 **to puzzle s.o.** to make s.o. feel confused – 24 **a joint answer** one answer for a number of questions – 25 **edgy** (*informal*) nervous – **fretty** (*informal for* fretful) uncomfortable – 26 **to be at a loose end** not to know what to do – **morose** [mə'rəʊz] unhappy and not talking very much – **morbid** having an interest in unpleasant things (e.g. death) – 28 **indolent** ['ɪndələnt] lazy

On heat? Randy? Full of desire? Full of energy? Full of dread? Drained? of energy, of dread? of desire?

Pause.

LAMB *[thinking]*: Well, it's difficult to say really …
PIFFS: Are you a good mixer?
LAMB: Well, you've touched on quite an interesting point there –
PIFFS: Do you suffer from eczema, listlessness, or falling coat?
LAMB: Er …
PIFFS: Are you virgo intacta?
LAMB: I beg your pardon?
PIFFS: Are you virgo intacta?
LAMB: Oh, I say, that's rather embarrassing. I mean in front of a lady –
PIFFS: Are you virgo intacta?
LAMB: Yes, I am, actually. I'll make no secret of it.
PIFFS: Have you always been virgo intacta?
LAMB: Oh yes, always. Always.
PIFFS: From the word go?
LAMB: Go? Oh yes, from the word go.
PIFFS: Do women frighten you?

She presses a button on the other side of her stool. The stage is plunged into redness, which flashes on and off in time with her questions.

PIFFS *[building]*: Their clothes? Their shoes? Their voices? Their laughter? Their stares? Their way of walking? Their way of sitting? Their way of smiling? Their way of talking? Their mouths?

1 **on heat** being ready for mating – **randy** sexually excited – **desire** [dɪzaɪə] strong wish (*here:* to have sex) – 2 **dread** [dred] feeling of great fear – 5 **a good mixer** s.o. who finds it easy to talk to people they do not know – 7 **eczema** ['eksɪmə] a skin disease (*Ekzem*) – **listlessness** a state in which a person has no energy or shows no enthusiasm – **falling coat** a mental disorder – 9 **virgo intacta** *(Latin)* woman (or man) who has not yet had sex – 18 **from the word go** *(informal)* from the very beginning – 22 **to be plunged into s.th.** *here:* to be completely covered with s.th. – **to flash** to shine brightly for a very short time – 25 **stare** long look at s.th. or s.o.

Their hands? Their feet? Their shins? Their thighs? Their knees? Their eyes?
Their *[Drumbeat]*. Their *[Drumbeat]*. Their *[Cymbal bang]*. Their *[Trombone chord]*. Their *[Bass note]*.

LAMB *[in a high voice]*: Well it depends what you mean really –

The light still flashes. She presses the other button and the piercing buzz-hum is heard again. LAMB's hands go to his earphones. He is propelled from the chair, falls, rolls, crawls, totters and collapses

Silence

He lies face upwards. MISS PIFFS looks at him then walks to LAMB and bends over him.

PIFFS: Thank you very much, Mr. Lamb. We'll let you know.

1 **shin** front part of the leg below the knee – **thigh** [θaɪ] top part of the leg between the knee and the hip – 3 **cymbal** ['sɪmbl] musical instrument in the form of a round metal plate, often two cymbals are hit together – 4 **trombone chord** [trɒm'bəʊn ˌkɔ:d] two or more notes played together by trombones, a brass musical instrument – 4 **bass note** [beɪs] low tone in music – 9 **to totter** to walk with unsteady steps

That's Your Trouble

Harold Pinter

Two men in a park. One on the grass, reading. The other making cricket strokes with umbrella.

A. *(stopping in mid-stroke)*: Eh, look at that bloke, what's he got on his back, he's got a sandwich board on his back.
B.: What about it?
A.: He wants to take it off, he'll get a headache.
B.: Rubbish.
A.: What do you mean?
B.: He won't get a headache.
A.: I bet he will.
B,: The neck! It affects his neck! He'll get a neckache.
A.: The strain goes up.
B.: Have you ever carried a sandwich board?
A.: Never.
B.: Then how do you know which way the strain goes? *(Pause.)* It goes down! The strain goes down, it starts with the neck and it goes down. He'll get a neckache and a backache.
A.: He'll get a headache in the end.
B.: There's no end.
A.: That's where the brain is.
B.: That's where the what is?
A.: The brain.
B.: It's nothing to do with the brain.
A.: Oh, isn't it?
B.: It won't go anywhere *near* his brain.
A.: That's where you're wrong.

2 **cricket stroke** the act of hitting a ball as in a game of cricket – 3 **bloke** (*BE; informal*) a man – 4 **sandwich board** (*BE*) a pair of boards with advertisements on them that s.o. wears at the front and back of their body as they walk around in public – 6 **he wants to** *(BE)* he needs to – 12 **strain** pressure – 20 **brain** organ inside the head that controls how you think, feel and move

B.: I'm not wrong. I'm right. *(Pause.)* You happen to be talking to a man who knows what he's talking about. *(Pause.)* His brain doesn't come into it. If you've got a strain, it goes down. It's not like heat.

A.: What do you mean?

B. *(ferociously)*: If you've got a strain it goes down! Heat goes up! *(Pause.)*

A.: You mean sound.

B.: I what?

A.: Sound goes up.

B.: Sound goes anywhere it likes! It all depends where you happen to be standing, it's a matter of physics, that's something you're just completely ignorant of, but you just try carrying a sandwich board and you'll find out soon enough. First the neck, then the shoulders, then the back, then it worms into the buttocks, that's where it worms. The buttocks. Either the right or the left, it depends how you carry your weight. Then right down the thighs – a straight drop to his feet and he'll collapse.

A.: He hasn't collapsed yet.

B.: He will. Give him a chance. A headache! How can he get a headache? He hasn't got anything on his head! I'm the one who's got the headache. *(Pause.)* You just don't know how to listen to what other people tell you, that's your trouble.

A.: I know what my trouble is.

B.: You don't know what your trouble is, my friend. That's your trouble.

6 **ferocious** [fəˈrəʊʃəs] aggressive, violent – 15 **to worm** [wɜːm] **into s.th.** to move slowly and with difficulty into s.th. – **buttocks** part of your body that you sit on – 17 **thigh** [θaɪ] top part of the leg between the knee and the hip – 18 **drop** fall

A Suite of Three Pieces

James Saunders*

W One of the things I like about being with you is that I don't feel obliged to talk all the time. It's easy to be silent with you. Being silent with you, close but not touching, eyes closed, not communicating with any of the five senses, just knowing you're there, feeling you're there, something else takes over, difficult to put into words because words belong to the five senses and this is something else. Something other. An awareness. It's hard to describe it. A feeling that you are somewhere inside me, I am somewhere inside you. Outside the senses, beyond time and space, outside ourselves. I can't put it into words. But it's there. Do you feel that?

M Hm?

W Do you feel that.

M I'm sorry, I wasn't listening.

W Here is an apple. See the apple. I want the apple. Do you want the apple?

M I want the apple. I also want you to have the apple.

W I also want you to have the apple. Shall we split the apple?

M But if we split the apple, we shall have nothing to argue about.

W Hey.

M Hm?

W Catch.

M Thanks.

W Eat.

M Catch.

W Thanks.

M Eat.

W Catch …

* * 1925 in London, worked as chemistry tutor (Southampton University) by day and wrote plays by night when he was young; wrote a number of well-known plays (*Next Time I'll Sing to You*, *A Scent of Flowers*); won a number of awards

suite [swi:t] a piece of music made up of related parts – 1 **to feel obliged to do s.th.** [ə'blaɪdʒd] to feel forced to do s.th. – 18 **to split** to cut into pieces

Up-To-Date

Shirley Ullom*

This is the greatest ... a dating service right in our own high school. All I have to do is fill out this simple form, pay five dollars, and a computer will match me up with a hunk ... a Prince Charming just waiting to wake me with a gentle kiss. That'll be soooo much better than holding slippery, sweaty hands with Freddy! I'm glad I had the guts to slip in here between classes. Wouldn't want any of my friends to find out. They said only a geekette would be stupid enough to let a computer choose her escort. I can imagine what Kisa Wilson would say: "Sara can't get a date any other way ... she has to pay for one!" Then she'd cut loose with that stupid little giggle of hers - tee hee, tee hee, tee heeeeee! Everybody would join in. If they didn't, she wouldn't invite them to her next party ... and everybody wants to be invited to Kisa's parties. Wall-to-wall food catered by the country club ... a band flown in from Chicago ... pictures taken for the front page of the yearbook! Well, that's why I came now so Kisa and the others won't find out. They have spies everywhere, but Ms. Young

* * 1938 in thc USA, writes sketches and monologues for young people to practise their dramatic abilities

1 **dating service** business that arranges meetings between single people who want to begin a relationship – 2 **to fill out** (*AE*) to fill in *(BE)* – 3 **to match s.o. up with s.o.** to connect s.o. with s.o. – **hunk** (*informal*) man who is big, strong and sexually attractive – **Prince Charming** (*usu. humorous*) the perfect boyfriend, the man a woman dreams of – 5 **slippery** used for s.th. difficult to grasp and hold because it is too smooth or wet – **sweaty** [swetɪ] *here:* wet, damp – 6 **guts** (*informal*) courage – 8 **geekette** [giːˈket] (*AE, informal*) female outsider who is seen as boring and unattractive – 9 **escort** [ˈeskɔːt] *here* (*old-fashioned*): man who takes a woman to a party and back home – 10 **to cut loose** [luːs] (*AE, informal*) to start doing s.th. in an uncontrolled way – 11 **giggle** [ˈgigl] silly, repeated laugh – 12 **to join in** to do the same – 14 **wall-to-wall** filling all the space between two walls – **to cater** to prepare and serve food for an event, etc. – 10 **yearbook** (*AE*) book published once a year in a school with information about what happened there in the year just passed – 17 **Ms.** [mɪz] a title that leaves open whether you are addressing an unmarried (Miss) or a married (Mrs.) woman

is in charge of this Computer Companionship Project … she'll keep it confidential.

Let's see … *(Reading)* "What are your interests?" Well, I like to read, watch sad movies and make corsages, but do I want a guy who wants to do those things? True, Freddy and I watched "Love Story" three times, but I'm here to find a dream date. Out with the old. I'd better just leave my interests blank. I read in *Totally Teen* that the popular girl is one whose interests match the guy she's with, so I'll just adapt to the big hunk the computer aims in my direction. I could learn to like football, duck hunting and car engines if my computer companion has a sexy smile! I know, I know, it's against our Forever Feminist by-laws, but these are troubled times and a girl's gotta do what a girl's gotta do … like pretending to be dumber than her date. Except with Freddy … we have the some GPA.

Now, this question is better: "What qualities am I looking for in a date?" Here we go … I want him to be kind to animals. I'll never forgive Todd Brennen for driving his Trans Am over Fluffy's tail. The poor kitty has a terrible time dragging its pancake tail up a tree! Of course, he'd have to be a good listener … they don't call me "the mouth" for nothing! Being courteous in front of my folks is a must … ever since Scott Tucker belched out "Jingle Bells" at the Christmas Eve dinner table, they've insisted on a manners code. Let's see, we got "go easy on the cat," "all ears when I speak," and "no belching Beethovens." Oh, brother, throw a towel over the poor schmuck's shoulders, paint an S on his chest and we have

2 **confidential** secret – 4 **corsage** [kɔːˈsɑːʒ] (*AE*) small bunch of flowers that is worn on a woman's dress, e.g. at a wedding – 6 **date** *here*: person one goes out with – 7 **blank** empty, without an entry (*Eintrag*) – ***Totally Teen*** magazine for teenagers – 9 **to adapt to s.o.** *here*: to change your behaviour in order to get along better with s.o. – 10 **duck hunting** *Entenjagd* – 12 **by-law** rule made by an organisation that applies to its members – 14 **dumb** [dʌm] stupid – 15 **GPA** (*AE*) short for: grade point average (*Notendurchschnitt*) – 18 **Trans Am** a type of American sports car – 21 **courteous** [ˈkɜːtɪəs] polite, respectful – 22 **to belch out** *here*: to burp *(rülpsen)* and sing at the same time – 23 **to insist on s.th.** to demand s.th. – **manners code** set of rules for how to behave correctly – 24 **to go easy on s.o.** (*informal*) to treat s.o. gently – **all ears** (*informal*) waiting with interest to hear what s.o. has to say – 26 **schmuck** [ʃmʌk] (*AE, informal, Yiddish origin*) a stupid person

Clark Kent in search of a phone booth! This questionnaire is too hard … and I thought today's geometry test was a challenge. I'll just leave that part blank.

"Where would you like to go on your first computer date?" That one should be easier. I'd like to go to a home game, a school play or even the junior/senior prom. Wait. What if this computer match-making magician fixes me up with a dog-faced Harry … a date that makes Frankenstein look like a Chippendale pin-up poster? I'd have to wear a veil … or my mom's wig on backwards. Freddy'll laugh, then he'll be bent out of shape like a super pretzel. He's been trying to get me to go to the prom with him. I'd better just leave this section blank, too.

I think I'm seeing a pattern here, and I'm beginning to get worried. I don't think I'm getting my five dollars' worth! How is the computer going to make a "love connection" if I keep leaving all the questions blank? It will probably match me up with a cucumber brain. Somebody too stupid to know the answers to these simple questions. Someone who is too chicken to fill in the blanks with two-syllable words. Someone who is going to forfeit their five bucks and get the heck out of here while nobody is looking. Oh, Freddy … Freddy. I've got good news about the prom …

1 **Clark Kent** name of an office clerk in a comic or film who sometimes turns into *Superman* to help others – 6 **prom** (*US, abbreviation of* promenade) the formal yearly high school dance – 7 **to fix s.o. up with s.o.** (*informal*) *jdn. mit jdm. verkuppeln* – 8 **Frankenstein** ['fræŋkənstaɪn] hero (monster) in Mary Shelley's novel – **Chippendale** one of a particular group of male strippers (the Chippendales) – 9 **veil** [veɪl] *Schleier* – **wig** a hairpiece – 10 **pretzel** *Brezel* – 13 **pattern** *here:* system – 17 **cucumber** ['kju:kʌmbə] *Gurke* – **cucumber brain** *here* (*informal*): s.o. with very low intelligence – 18 **chicken** (*informal*) afraid – 19 **to forfeit** ['fɔ:fɪt] to lose – 20 **buck** (*AE, informal*) dollar – **(the) heck** (*informal*) exclamation of emphasis

Vocabulary and exercises

This collection of vocabulary will help you talk and write about sketches and mini-dramas. It is presented in thematic sections so that you can easily find expressions which are useful for the sketch or the task you are dealing with:

1 dramas/plays
2 sketches and mini-dramas
3 action and plot
4 characters
5 language
6 humour
7 performing a sketch
8 responding to a sketch

In between the sections, you will find additional questions and tasks, which will require you to work with a specific section of the vocabulary.

Check yourself - Basic vocabulary defined in context

What basic drama vocabulary do you already know?
Do this self-check activity to find out.
Fill in the gaps with these 16 essential words:

actresses – acts – audience – cast – critic –dialogues – directions – director – performance – play – playwright – props – rehearsals – review – roles – scenes

The author of a ... (or drama) is called a .... A play usually consists of several ... which can be subdivided into ....
The ... or parts are played by ... and actors, who make up the .... The characters talk to each other in ....
The ... helps the actors and actresses to put the stage ... (where to stand, how to move and speak) into practice and decides about the use of ... (furniture or objects on the stage).
The actors and actresses practice putting on the play during .... Finally, they put on the play for the public in a ....
The people who watch the play are called the ....
A ... expresses her or his view of the quality of a performance in a ....

1 dramas/plays

basic elements of **drama:** themes, intentions, setting (place and time of action), action, plot, characters, language

playwrights/dramatists/authors have different intentions for their **plays:** for example to make you smile or laugh (**comedy**) or make you feel pity with one or more of the characters because they suffer a downfall (**tragedy**).

a play ...

- is set in a certain location (**setting**) which creates a specific atmosphere
- appeals to the emotions of the audience
- may delight the spectators
- may arouse pity or evoke fear
- deals with/treats a theme or a topical issue and my instruct the audience

2 sketches and mini-dramas (two types of plays) ...

- are very short ("playlets") and self-contained
- consist of one scene only (with a beginning, a middle and an end)
- usually take place in only one setting
- have a limited number of characters
- aim to entertain
- are primarily intended to be perormed as part of a theatre show (a revue) or on TV with playlets, jokes, songs and dances

a sketch ...

- is mostly humorous
- is as a rule based on the quick exchange of remarks
- ends with a punchline (a final twist)
- may refer to recent events

typical **aspects of sketches**: outsiders, mistaken identity, strange or extreme behaviour, exaggeration, absurdities, confusion, slapstick, incompetence, cruelty

a mini-drama ...
- is generally serious
- uses ordinary or everyday language
- shows the deeper or symbolic meaning of everyday life
- frequently seems to begin and end at some arbitrary point, thus giving the impression of being open-ended

Mini-dramas typically contain realistic characters, deal wirh everyday incidents or problems (e.g. communication problems) and contain aspects of social criticism.

---

3 action and plot

Action refers to the sequence of happenings in a play.
Plot refers to more than the series of events: an analysis of the plot shows how events are arranged and related to one another (cf. flashbacks, repetitions, foreshadowing, etc.) and why things happen.

The action...
- takes place in a single setting
- rises/moves to a crisis
- reaches a turning point
- reveals the development of a conflict between the caracters
- begins/ends abruptly

The plot ...
- is simple/straightforward, intricate or complex
- may be well organized or confusing
- unfolds in the course of the sketch or mini-drama

---

4 characters

– main/leading and minor characters
– protagonist, antagonist
– to be in conflict with opponents
– to give a speech/to deliver a monologue/to whisper an aside
– to address another character/to overhear a conversation/ to enter into a dialogue with ...

---

5 language

- dialogue (conversation between two or more people)
- aside (words which only the audience are supposed to hear)
- monologue (long speech)
- soliloquy (speech given by a character alone on stage to reveal thoughts, emotions and motives)
- silence
- body language
- lines/passages of lively dialogue/repartee (i.e. clever and amusing comments, quick replies)
- everyday/colloquial/informal language

The language reveals the nature of a character/determines the **tone** of the sketch. The following adjectives can be used to describe the tone of the sketch: friendly, polite, encouraging, playful, witty, serious; unfriendly, impolite, ironic, satirical, sarcastic, provocative, angry, threatening, rude

6 humour

Humour is the quality of being entertaining or amusing. Humour may be achieved through various devices. Nations and people may differ in their sense of humour.

- to appreciate/share s.o.'s sense of humour
- situational/verbal humour
- deadpan/dry humour
- subtle/infectious humour
- to amuse/entertain the audience
- to make fun of s.o., to ridicule s.o., to laugh at/about s.th.
- to have/produce/create/achieve a humorous/comic effect
- to provoke/induce laughter

In pairs, compare your sense of humour by finding out what you and your partner find or do not find amusing, funny, laughable, ridiculous or silly.
Based on what you have read or seen in the media or experienced in real life, do you think there are national differences in what people consider funny? If your answer is yes, what are the differences?

devices to create humorous effects

- **stock characters:** characters who lack complexity and embody/personify a particular idea (compare: flat/round characters in fiction); stock characters are based on **stereotypes,** i.e. generalized ideas about a certain kind of person or group of people (e.g. sexual, ethnic or professional stereotypes)
- **verbal devices**
  black humour: anecdotes/jokes which are intended to amuse by making fun of the unpleasant aspects of life, e.g. murder, death, etc.
  euphemism: a more gentle expression used instead of the usual one to express unpleasant, frightening or embarrassing facts (e.g. *pass away* for *die*)
  hyperbole: a statement which is exaggerated
  irony: saying one thing but meaning the opposite
  pun: a play on words; puns are constructed around a word which has two different meanings so that a sentence can be understood in two different ways
  sarcasm: a remark which is cutting and meant to hurt
  understatement: the opposite of hyperbole – when something is represented as being less important than it really is
- **physical devices**
  slapstick: a phrase which refers to the use of exaggerated physical action to amuse the audience, e.g. hitting, kicking, throwing things at one another and falling down
- **verbal and/or physical devices**
  parody: copying or imitating the style of something or someone in an exaggerated way

---

In pairs, write a fictitious interview with a famous director on the use of humour in films and on television.

7 performing a sketch

- to give a (public) performance
- to stage/perform a sketch
- to practise/rehearse a sketch, to have/hold a rehearsal
- dress rehearsal (final practice)

Stage directions provide information about entrances or exits, the setting, body language, silences, pauses, the tone of speaking, etc.

the stage:

- the curtain (rises, falls), properties (props), scenery
- director, actors, actresses. prompter

actors and actresses ...

- play a major/minor part/role in a play
- are members of the cast
- enter/leave the stage
- make their entrance from the left/right
- rehearse a play
- wear costumes and make-up

Your favourite actor or actress looks back on his or her first experiences on stage. Collect ideas and write a statement about his or her experiences, then "perform" it live in front of the class and let them guess who you are impersonating. What you say need not be true but should still be typical of the actor/actress you have chosen.

8 responding to a sketch
- a laughable/ridiculous/humorous character

the audience/spectators
- to applaud/boo a performance
- to break out into laughter
- to roar with laughter
- to be convulsed with laughter
- to burst into tears of laughter
- to find a performance/a remark/a punchline extremely/highly amusing
- to be amused at/by s.th.
- to chuckle: to laugh quietly when thinking about s.th. funny
- to titter/to giggle: to laugh in a nervous, embarrassed or silly way
- to roar: to laugh very loudly

A critic writes a review of a performance/a sketch revue.
- to review a performance
- to receive bad/unflattering/mixed reviews
- to receive favourable/ecstatic reviews

A sketch revue with several of the sketches from this collection is to be reviewed in your school magazine or local paper. Write this review. You can make this review either favourable or critical, or you can give a mixed response to the performances.

Acknowledgements

Jest a Moment
from *The Penguin Dictionary of Jokes*; compiled and edited by Fred Metcalf, Penguin Books, London, 1994; pp. 52, 194

The Question Game
from THE HOLT GUIDE TO ENGLISH 2/E 2nd edition by IRMSCHER W. © 1976. Reprinted with permission of Heinle, a division of Thomson Learning: www.thomsonrights.com. Fax 800 730-22 15

Useless, but High Paying by Kirk Buis
from *Comedy Duets* #4, © copyright 1990 Meriwether Publishing Ltd., USA, pp. 13–16, used by permission

Fatal Beatings by Ben Elton and Richard Curtis
quoted from *Short and Sweet – Short texts and how to use them* (vol. 2) by Alan Maley; Penguin Books, London, 1995; pp. 128–128

American Welcome by Brian Friel
from *More Ten-Minute Plays from Actors Theatre of Louisville*, ed. by Michael Bigelow Dixon; Samuel French; © 1981 by Brian Friel; pp. 105–109

Hospital Flash by Courtney Hope
from *Footlight Fun Encore*, J. Garnet Miller Ltd., Malvern, 1963; pp. 43–45

On the Pier by Courtney Hope
from *Footlight Fun Encore*, J. Garnet Miller Ltd., Malvern, 1963; pp. 40–42

There's No Witch at the Hilton by Peg Kehret
from *Comedy Duets* #2 © copyright 1973 Meriwether Publishing Ltd., USA, pp. 1–6, used by permission

Honest Abe – Can He Stay That Way? by Bill Majeski
from *Doubletalk – Fifty Comedy Duets for Actors* © copyright 1990 Meriwether Publishing Ltd., USA, pp. 72–75, used by permission

The Subway Werewolf by Richard Mauro
from *Variety Show Comedy Skits* © copyright 1989 Meriwether Publishing Ltd., USA, pp. 10–11, used by permission

Devil of an Interview by Daron Scott McFarland
from *Duos and Trios* © copyright 1999 Meriwether Publishing Ltd., USA, pp. 19–22, used by permission

The Applicant by Harold Pinter
from *Plays – Three*, Methuen, 1986 (1978); pp. 231–234

That's Your Trouble Applicant by Harold Pinter
from *Plays – Three*, Methuen, 1986 (1978); pp. 227–228

A Suite of Pieces by James Saunders
from James Saunders, *Games and After Liverpool*; Samuel French, London, 1973; pp. 8, 13

Up-To-Date by Shirley Ullom
from *Chitchat* © copyright 1992 Meriwether Publishing Ltd., USA, pp. 5–6, used by permission